RED JUICE

Wave Books
Seattle and New York

HOA NGUYEN

Red Juice

POEMS 1998–2008

Published by Wave Books

www.wavepoetry.com

Wave Books titles are distributed to the trade by

Consortium Book Sales and Distribution

Phone: 800-283-3572 / SAN 631-760X

Library of Congress Cataloging-in-Publication Data

Nguyen, Hoa.

[Poems Selections]

Red juice : poems, 1998–2008 / Hoa Nguyen. — First edition.

pages cm

ISBN 978-1-933517-93-3 (Limited edition hardcover)

ISBN 978-1-933517-92-6 (Trade paperback)

I. Title.

PS3614.G88A6 2014

811'.6–dc23

2013041147

Designed and composed by Quemadura

Printed in the United States of America

9 8 7 6 5 4 3 2 1

First Edition

For Dale

YOUR ANCIENT SEE THROUGH

ONION HEAD I HAVE

THE TRILLIONTH DAY OF DNA

RED JUICE

HECATE LOCHIA

INTRODUCTION

I've been reading Hoa Nguyen's poems since the mid-1990s, when we were both part of an informal collection of writers and artists living and working in San Francisco & pushing ourselves "to regain authority for the innate coherence of whatever it is that we propose as life," to borrow a turn from Robert Creeley. Not that any of us would have said so with such particularity (or not been horrified to have it put that way at all). It was a down-home set of overlapping circles, not without mercurial temperament and various spirited indulgences, and we were, I think, decidedly invested in what we took to be our differences in source & material as points of departure. The question of what there was to know, in any given experience of a piece of writing, fueled our conversations, chaotic and casual as they may have felt at the time.

Immediately apparent inside Nguyen's poetry, to me at least, was a command of voice as an ongoing structural phenomenon, built through diction and velocity while giving off an implicit belief in the agency of a life and the agency of a poem, at once. I've stayed with her work ever since (by 1996 she was off to Austin, Texas, where she'd live and work for over a decade and a half), following the poems through their various arrangements in books and chapbooks published by a range of more-or-less fugitive presses: Leroy, Mike & Dale's, the subpress collective, effing press, Hot Whiskey, and Dos Press, chronologically speaking. The work collected herein originally resided in the publications these presses crafted with terrific care between 1998 and 2008, as well as in numerous magazines and anthologies, and represent the bulk of Nguyen's work prior to the release of *As Long as Trees Last* in 2012.

I experience Nguyen's poems as sonic environments made word by word, provoked by lived experience into forms that, as she figures it, "press out and in." I take that in part to mean a refusal to lean on material outside the particulars of the work, which is all the more inviting for said refusal. The fluidity of the poems, their apparent quickness, nearly belies Nguyen's ability to be continuously decisive (what I mean by command) while deploying via breaks, cuts, & spaces in her lines a patterning of sound amplified by a direct emphasis on where pauses should fall. Phrase by phrase Nguyen's work can be conversational, playful, funny, angry, acutely self-aware, and loaded with sensory information. The poems' accrual of emotional significance (an aspect of their form) is evenly distributed among points of consciousness and their attendant pressures: the continuous need to assert the oddity of action that makes up a self; the necessary figuring and refiguring of love and intimacy in a shared space; bringing babies who become children with their own relationships to language into that space ("Would you like a K sandwich?"); anxiety about money, time, work, art, family, upbringing, the question of fate, the murkiness of origin; resistance to the notion of permanent war as a public, domestic, agreed-upon mind frame in which to take part, while reckoning nonetheless with the body counts.

Inside a collection of work made largely of shorter poems the points of emphasis are many, due in large part to Nguyen's attention to minute particulars in combination with an insistence on treating each particular as a released possibility, passing through the relative time of its utterance in order to briefly hold and give way. Dreams, lists, overheard snippets of conversation, judgments ("Hating my needing to be loved"), rituals for attracting money, and an innate feel for scale and locale are among Nguyen's many sources for the materials of the poems, everything present and exact in an available and nonetheless idiosyncratic diction. Her terms obey no fashion, being subject only to the conviction of her artistic perception. All of this detail, spirit, and commitment to the art makes for a great deal of pleasure, a value poetry remains capable of asserting, in time, at high and ordinary levels of consciousness, irrespective of mess and message.

Anselm Berrigan

YOUR ANCIENT SEE THROUGH

ONION HEAD I HAVE

[BUDDHA'S EARS ARE DROOPY TOUCH HIS SHOULDERS]

Buddha's ears are droopy   touch his shoulders
as scarves fly out of windows and I shriek
at the lotus of enlightenment

Travel to Free Street past Waco
to the hole in the Earth
wearing water

I'm aiming my mouth
for apple pie

BAKED ALASKA

It is possible   You can
take whole parts of land   chunk
of ice cream (pink)   ice cream
mysterious meringue
Stuff it in a hot box   hot   How
is the trick of it   baking
igloos with kin inside
They are they   not real   ice
cream   white and pink
It's complicated

[FIND & FUND IT'S A PRISON OVEN]

Find & fund   It's a prison oven
(U.S.)   sterilized and smells good like
chemicals   engines   manufactured
houses
          Hey vingpie!
I'm great and so are you
grooving on Armageddon gas
where therapy is tomorrow's lover's lane
                    Pupipara
Groove in a boob tube

[BAD BEATS IT SAYS NOW "COME ON IN]

bad beats it says now "come on in
come on in" make snowmen (women) of the white page
onion head I have (go in) favorites
of my father my never-had brother leaning
over a car engine greasy I was the mess
Carl What was I doing gazing at cleft chins
punching boys because I was so mad!

[I'M ALMOST YOUR CAT'S PAJAMAS]

I'm almost your cat's pajamas
your topsy turvy all over
almost a pinup of yarnballs
at the rest-stop of undeclared wars
(the way Descartes faked it)
give me history or give me
a name unknown in zoology
So I can be anything but empty doll
all jammed body doll   a pregnancy
to be "natural"

LOZENGE

There's a revolution going on
and commercials & football on TV
Secret
river in the sky   it's a tree or crocodile
Mayans say it ends in 12 years
(sky fall down)

layer   layer   layer

I could be born graceful
to pull turnips or rice
or tricks all my life
long wavy hair   plump lips

and then die
The secret seed of the thing

Bulbing words
throb the way hearts do

VIEW

What we don't know supports what
we know   we don't know
anything—the principal animal
as in ritual   we eat dinner
early sausages   beef in the Four Seasons
Hotel   neighbor to a damned lake
(flooded river valley)   we are the principal
animal   toasting ourselves on the stuffed
sofa   where I am   The buffalo
is the image of death   remains
remind

BOX OF BUTTER

Indian girl vaguely
white   hands holding
the product box   forever
repeating image of her
on the product box
in her hands   cut it up
and fold the girl
Make breasts of her knees

[MULBERRY MESS SQUISH SQUASH]

Mulberry mess   squish squash
I give tree names   The land has names
I'm finding them   Who are you with your white
beard?
        Turned into a tree

The hill offers a sky bowl

We are wow   but I'm thinking
the planet turns & there was a war
He said "Kill yesterday" when
           he was
               tall and laughing and cruelly

        The ground turned to blood
Sweet with green sour stems

[THE YELLING FATHER MAKES METERED BABIES]

The yelling father makes metered babies
tick   tick   I'm evil
the terrible peace of my creepy
lies   shut your down mouth
all beat   & up the awkward stairs
makes me evil   disturbs you
Put a papal pin on it

A STORY OF HISTORY

You shall hear the story
You shall hear the story how Pau-Puk-Keewis danced
at Hiawatha's wedding
The student cried "Hurrah!"
The student cried "Now you have it!"
I must have more light
I must have what I asked for
Your presence will not be necessary

I WOKE UP THIS MORNING AND IT WAS FRIDAY

Scribbling aimlessly and abstractedly on scraps of paper
my life is completely uninteresting
to you, Dear Reader   "O I guess
I have a mother now"

Pretend I am asleep
                                        Hang up!

She struggles to carry the flowers
up the stairs

If only the world wasn't glob-al
"Don't be a sucker"

[UNORTHODOX & IMPRACTICAL ONE NOT LED]

Unorthodox & impractical   one not led
easily and conceals my greed under
friendliness   I am a tiger wife
a tiger in each knee   like silent
pissed off Kaufman   I am guilty
I am tragic   I must die   being
Ho Chi Minh & Groucho Marx and also
Isadora Duncan

THE TRILLIONTH DAY OF DNA

SMELL THE PURPLE INCENSE THAT MAY OR MAY NOT SMELL BETTER THAN THE RAT YOU NAME "COMPOSITION"

Winter fails   You drive
a motorcycle around it!
The difference in today is
                        a Valentine zit

"You have your whole life ahead of you
except for the part you've already lived"

                                    Calmly   la la
your swirly clothesline habits

            Why can't I have glitter toes?

Magic lifts my hair   (That's the wind)

RITUAL FOR ATTRACTING MONEY

1. Act like you're a snobby goose
2. Buy groceries that are green colored
3. Braid your hair with golden ribbons
   and sleep with gold ribbons in your hair
4. Look at birds over your left shoulder
5. Walk with a cane very slowly
   saying "Hmm . . ."

POPPIES

Poppies for sleep   Poppies for your highway
at Ben Lomon or Los Gatos   Poppies for your
Charles Baudelaire eyedrops   Poppies
to please my red field of vision   Poppies
for a lemon cake   Poppies smack you on
the head   Poppies that are closed and
poppies that are open   Plastic poppies discontinued
at Hobby Lobby   Poppies in a glass jar
on your bed-stand   Remember-the-dead poppies

[SITTING THERE NEARLY TRANSLUCENT YOU'LL END UP]

Sitting there nearly translucent   You'll end up
having to bury him   Higher elevations
are cold make your lips turn blue

I sat in a tree with a wire star
the kind you find at the last minute

"memories"

Poppies that fade as bright as that
rubbing plastic beads against your teeth

(inward now)

The cave the dancer made

"Flowers for ritual or medicine"

[BABY I'VE DRAWN YOUR FACE]

Baby I've drawn your face
underwater like an iceberg
The ice-blue clear kind
A perfect frozen eyeball

I cried   I made flowers grow
an offering   little "o"s
for kisses   want to kiss
the air tonight   See thru and blue

[A NIGHT AT THE BEACH WHAT IS LEFT]

A night at the beach   what is left
conch shell   shimmer marks
where feet trail across sand
dense as stars   Humans like me
can't hear beneath the trillionth
day of DNA   sung meaning
of sea waves   Sting nettle
having waves to paddle

[FLYING COLORS LAND DIVIDE A PLACE   YOU]

Flying colors land   divide a place   You
have this I'll take it   swirl like a
target radar eye   I am a crowned bird
on a pointy nest   the monster next door
crowned bird on a pointed nest where
we're from two colors   two maps
dividing land   ugly lots
garden variety ones

ROSY

can't be writing poems not scribbled
cats   my love adoring and why
to trim the plants
with pink footstool   pink handled scissors
"massage the data"   so when curled
neck massage makes dreams
management systems"   me tenderly
be   "enterprise solutions for municipal
is dull   in language as work is or can

FOB

boredom with food   create pasta!
minutes   it is not impossible to be sexual
so when curled after 13
chains in the tongue chain   wowie
enterprise solutions"   language as work dulls
my tweaky adoring dreams "for municipal

HORSE SONG

Where else to be
stabbing a two headed Pegasus
    breathing flower fire before my delicates

I am hidden in the trunk
        with your flower essences
I am a stickler about applications
I apply the tincture to my mouth hurts
            My delicate lung trees

My too strong back and lousy photograph
        Lunging for the air singing

[RIDE A BIKE TO HOUSTON]

Ride a bike to Houston
ride and put your foot down
on the pedal   unlike a flower
ride my name out   Stop
calling me Oriental   Rick Wallace
Ride for the Saturnalia
that I always sister
Clang and traffic-ing cars
that will be the death of us

[WHAT CAN BE MY DISOBEY]

What can be my disobey
the kettle song   split morning
too much coffee and all the guilt
in my consumer kit

Veg out   think think

Your baby thoughts
are typical for your class
            and your education level

[I LIKE THE LIGHT BLUE]

with John Keats, Bernadette Mayer, and Edwin Denby

I like the light blue with your dark slacks not
Long distance family pains & work work work
"Want me a tough love seat with firm pillows"
Touch has a memory   O say, love, say

It's a cosmic shuffle you've broken into
Papaver Eraticum Rubrum
Like the moon's reply, the bayed moon
Friends smiling   stepping out the door

Bring specific flowers I will not know the names of
Slowly pump your arms as you walk by
I do and it is dull if you won't call
The day is gone and sweets are gone

Like the moon, like your mom: fly children
The light and shade—a sort of black brightness

PINK BRIDGE

[UNTOUCHED BUBBLE GUM ME]

Untouched bubble gum me
          fruity and whole
Scream wrapped in plastic
Sling your barbells in the air

Seismic nervous falling
(walking the fence   no hands)

Pink bubble gum doll wrapped
in purple coveralls
running away
dragging the family piano

MNEMOSYNE

tracing the pink fading as a hand
print exactly because it was   the thin
cotton had embroidered slowly as
your mother's fine crimson   the crisp

leaves wouldn't cut a hand being she looked
at it   rendered in thread   but your back was
turned doodling roses on a notebook
funny how the innocent night gown

taking it out you don't remember what
it was you didn't stitch   most
likely see through light blue garbage chore
maybe complicated flowers not

taking it out he came up from behind
surprising like that and your mother joined
you in the bathroom to see to say nothing
is the matter really as it fades there

[PINK BRIDGE HEARTS THAT LOOK LIKE]

Pink bridge   hearts that look like
flank steak   my 3 fingers span
a pink landscape where women
sing bendly   croon brown bundles
Ribbons of red for streaming
placenta blood   the strength card
where queens subdue lions
I thump my fist through
tangle puzzle parts ,   pull
wayward angel yards

SHRED

we are complicating
patterns.   destiny

            is a big room.   we talk
like jets missing

home: a view of sky as a child
a cotton diorama.

birds collect where they will
telephone wire.   the front stoop.

what days aren't pinched by absence

we are here
in our skin.   destiny

            is a small city
I could die today.

[PAUSE RATE THE FALL]

Pause rate the fall
Climb the hill fall back down

(Barney coloring books
on a giant web-press
puts eyes in impossible purple)

Watch as nouns pile up
piled in the thingified air

whirling sirens
telephone posts
post post-village
Office Depot

[HARD TOFU
WHAT TO EAT TODAY]

hard tofu   what to eat today
We are well fed   fresh greens
donate my organs for the next
life, Doctor   take medicine
corruption   It's MTV meets
my mom

[HOUSE ON FIRE MY MOM'S]

house on fire   my mom's
past house   a child   she
lost the tea pot shaped
from a big hard fruit
Gone too the rain
trees   how they curved
in to bring water
for store   (drink)   wash
in the river

[UNDERWATER FLOWER]

Underwater Flower
put your Thumbelina there
where her winter of damage
is dressed in chronic crap rags
(underground with a mole man)
                    Teach your daughters
the mad man stance
Add accessories   carry bath salts.

OFFING

What your dark eyes take back
to itself, hugged in a curve
of toughness. The land between us is flat.
Let's say we are ruined, Minneapolis,
bricked against ourselves. A red rag
in the kitchen. This isn't important or I am.

I never wanted to touch you
and still do. How can we pray or find
what collects in heaven, Father?
I'd be surprised by elegance,
meaning something like rugs
and leather. Soft and tough. This.

I want belief like this. Leaving
the sea is a rag doll I once was. Texas
clouds in dreams, swinging. My loving you
once, mud puddle, swing set.

[CRASS AND BURN YOUR TERRIBLE]

Crass and burn   your terrible
mouth corner   little sour spot
like something   like something
compared to something
Parrot drum   Living it

[COLD BLACK LITTLE PUDDLE STOPS]

Cold black   little puddle stops
I can't help stopping   make wild cat
Pledges

          O piano solo   cello solo
Long low beat of living

                    Places I want to go for
myself   ancient with horrible pockets

[JEALOUS ALL THE PISSY THINGS]

Jealous   all the pissy things
hating the name Oscar
I should drip blue
heavy chi and the vortex between tables

Selfish I should say
birds and
their selfish flying
          porous O above the bridge
for me

MISSION DOLORES

Stream of our Lady of Sorrows
Dolores   though the river is gone now
          Ring your bell on holy days   sunny
Mission and the old cemetery
in the District of Missions

     Palmy Dolores
bright ceiling dim with candle smoke
survivor of earthquakes and fires
(Dolores and her gold fire hydrant)

$1 will get you history
          museum entry and a California moment
Dolores where I kissed you
          for a lifetime wishing fierceness
to die with you or maybe
                         just after you

''LAST PIECES''

TIME OUT FROM THE HAZARD GARDEN & INSTANTANEOUS BALONEY

for Rachel Loden

I wish I had Candy Land pants
Smear sweat   nuzzle the cat
I'm smug and well fed
                                        Pat my stomach in public
flatten the napkin and malarkey conversations
Mind the squiggle
"Rain can be too much or too little"
Not being able to eat my noodles
DISAFFECTED AND DEAD
I am the public I brush up against

18-YEAR-OLD KURT COBAIN ARRESTED FOR PAINTING "HOMOSEXUAL SEX RULES" ON THE SIDE OF AN ABERDEEN BANK: POLICE REPORT OF POCKET CONTENTS

a guitar pick
a key
a beer
a mood ring and
a cassette
by the militant punk band
Millions of Dead Cops

[CATS UNDERWATER   A ZOO]

Cats underwater as part of a zoo
tableau   orange tabby cats
sad wet fur   They blink
so rarely   moldy necks
My sister doesn't feel anything
I was wearing the old black hat
on the subway   when I saw the old lover
I think he has a "lard ass"

FROM A NY TIMES REVIEW OF KLEMPERER'S 1942–1945 DIARY

Surrender radio and telephone
also give up theater   movies   concerts
libraries
then no more magazines or newspapers
no more Jews on buses   no sitting on trams
finally no trams—except to distant forced labor
no more tobacco   flowers   milk
also no more haircuts
turn in the typewriter   also furs   blankets
fabrics
no more biking
now kill the cat and all other pets
no walking on such-and-such streets   no storing food
at home
no eating at restaurants   no clothing card   no fish card
just one hour a day for shopping
turn in all appliances   keys   metals
lamps

DREAM 5.22.97

Skimming a lake   The Beloved Lake   pooled
with viscous oil   flamingos drowned
long pick necks   pink curling
towards bellies   On the Vegas steamboat
I clamor stairs   up   down   past slots   wheels
lights light neon   On the deck
I lean over the lake   take up the slick
from the spilled tanker   in a slot machine
quarter's cup   like fat from a soup
            More flamingos dancing
drowned in the wake of our passing
and I think (desperate now) I will at last
find a job

SPECKLED

like roses

someone smells

me   cubicles away   roses

the smell of stinking faux

I don't really like

shoes   sometimes

too   I sprinkle in my

like roses   rose powder

roses   my lotion smells

[MEAN SUDDENLY BITCH WOMAN]

Mean suddenly   Bitch woman
scolding the kids cutting through
the yard   Stick out your arm
for the fuck you salute   Bend into
duck lips   I scratch little
rivulets   Shake it little sluggard
Dress me in watermelon green
I want to dance putrid   shout
rub out the Y dividing line

CAPTIVE AND ABLE

Bells gathered like bells   What are
captive and able   thin clapper clapping
cast in a bell   in a jealous bell

I am a gatherer in the jealous bell
the ugly tangent cast in a race
(divergently)   I am so unfair

sometimes   believing the bells
and jealous of someone else

TO PASS

Wagon   red wagon   rust of course   your overlapping toes
on curled edge   I'm back pulling *Advertisers*
every Wednesday   for to have   for to have   fold
the newsprint   sister I slap you   I am sister
older   playing tricks   yank you down sidewalks
whining in the red wagon   stop for a sunset
we're suddenly beautiful   pretending we are
Hawaiians delivering *Advertisers*

SPEAKING WHEN SPOKEN TO

Mother is a cookie cutter, an attached lid
shut. The little ones escaped
outside.   Skip.   Flip.   Attack
one another with cart-wheels.
Father is running. You were clever
to look like a machine.
Home, our small beds,
something else reeling us in.   I hung
hair, stood on my head, we were good fish.
You talk to them like you talk to them
on the phone.   We say a few words.

[MONSTER MADE YOU WERE]

Monster made   you were
To sing and blaze because
issue quickened how my glory is
your little feet   chrysanthemums
that made me hate sister blood
I hated you for you wouldn't hush
burgeoned from peaceable jingles
Lucky Dog   yours is a mouth

[LET'S SEE IF SHE'LL RUN AWAY]

Let's see if she'll run away
or let the kite eat them
Mom wearing waitress whites
Flees from you on playground mulch
Runs past the fake rocket
away from you   Howl for her
          howl anyway
Secretly know why
she cuts her hair short

[YEARS AFTER STEALING CATTLE FROM THE WOMB]

Years after stealing cattle from the womb
your face is slightly smeary

The globe cracks and depends on you

All the elements literally "at my feet"
pointing in a disco dance stance
where two waters (dry beds) divide
I wear a simple pin and dirty jeans

A strong dancer that leaps ahead
to sing "Last Pieces"

ROSE PATCH

[YOU HAVE YOUR ANCIENT SEE THROUGH]

You have your ancient see through
ways   Stars sustain their axis
Orion listing like gallows
for my creepy life   the pieces
of our ascending selves

        Olmecs
        (save a few stone faces)
        erased in the '50s by an oil company

Bleeping gastro kick-start
We pock mark plains

DARK

then owl
yellow-eyed   black pupil

this is a body going numb from will
meeting the outside world   forehead

where the feathers were   she blinks   Athene
how your wisdom darkens   makes

trouble for me to see in the eye's center
grapple after life's cog—anima—

special where rain is caught
on the tongue   now my left hand is

numb where the knowledge knife is gifted
and owl nimble-necked blinks at me   certain

SOME DUMB LOVE

Dive or stay you were red your shirt was
though I took home its stripes as tangent
material red-love What were you
looming distant ardent lover Why did you gather
me (your restaurant arms) Why trace our distance
now? I am weird for you your redness
escapes me my draping (dreams)
your arms all around

HESITATING WINTER

In the corner near the window
the North wind blows cold
Please give us ice cream
with roses large thorned and small
leaves swinging on the gate
Here comes the procession
mingled with the odor of withered flowers
and packing our lunch
today   I longed to see a flower   Coward
Cowards   how we dread that name

[STAYING AT WORK FOR LUNCH]

Staying at work for lunch
Eat an apple   no shoes on
Or cats that talk by a bed

Bring in bats please   neon blue
Unavailable weather means no socks

Make me cry in a dumb cube
Well fuck you too

[EXHAUSTION BREAK THROUGH CHALLENGES]

Exhaustion break through challenges
it's a swirling sea then calm where
clashing rocks spell moist alarm
& life's absurd toad flaunts its nose
Nine for the bird-boat flags
Nine for the wand-raised hill
Nine for the stone steps crossed
I create you   still push hard

[PASTEL LAPEL PRETEND ERASE]

Pastel lapel   Pretend Erase
your name on God's ledger
for to seek in the guise of wise
plaining   Meteor is my name
and purple skies tonight

CALM IN THE VEGETABLE BEARD OF TIME

His golden ear-loops cover
handsome honed cheek bones
with wonder   My-eyed wonder at
gazing   him   speechless   nearly
no mouthed beneath the varying
grey green blue   of his wise chin

Dots   Dots or a ladder connect us
Insect antennae   antennae under water
as in crawfish whisker carp   Speckled
forehead wrinkles at Rilke when I say "Beauty
is nothing but the beginning of terror"
Laugh   Shake your head   I saw
noses first   felt my own   the issuing
spot through which I begin and begin again

[INTERLOCKING PROFILES]

Interlocking profiles
how the mouth protrudes
through the other's face
faces joined like vases
smiling lips   nostril x
or a vest with two buttons
has become of union
double secret grin
up-turning chin

[LOOK ON THE DAMNED LAKE]

Look on the damned lake
          He was not home
or perhaps was dead
My father's house on huge pile stilts
as if the ground had shrunken up
               Swaying underside and sub-floor
where kitchen-rug dust repels
the family I was
     ½ conscious of

The water must be salty
after performing an initiation drama
          a short short performance that
disappoints the audience in the open
kitchen where I sit in what is
     formally called a breakfast nook

I am done and chapped with fault
   say to the in-tide as the house rocks
"I *will* not put a rose patch
on your lapel in the basement."

[TORTURED FIRE AND FOOT HELD]

Tortured   fire and foot held
You're held in a fever passion
holding the filcher of alder ember

Sneak fire in a fennel stalk
(narthex)

                    Beater of anvils
are you afraid to put your
tortilla in the fire?   No
I use a pan

          Forethought
          Fetters
          Yellow
          Burn
          New Power
          The prince of love dungeons

She said, "You're living   aren't you?"

GREY

From the fog of your window
you cry for moss covered fishes
sticks of bacon gone bad   anything
that rings the haze from the sky
A boom of smoke where the land is
on fire   no rain all month
now rain washing your shitty car

THE TEA IS YOU
YOU ARE THE TEA

near the ruins of this hour
no longer
all
phenomenon
goes and wash
in linking waves
it is not the object seen
ruining my blue coat
go and tell somebody
returning to your true hour:
it is dark outside
it is dark in my mouth
the sun makes me burn

[ROLL IN YOUR SKULL GONE GREEN]

Roll in your skull gone green
like a mossy cog that wings
Sing the good times
You seem a tiny wrecked thing to me
something sacred   where time has gone
old and green   Norse
hymns bringing dawn

LET'S EAT RED FOR FUN

[LOVE CALLS FOR HADES COLD CREAM]

Love calls for Hades cold cream
Love talks in picture code
          and Valentines

Let's eat red for fun
                    eat tragicomedies

Epic red-love
washes all Valentines
          and gets my shoes wet

Like worn addled Valentines saying
"Sorry about Janice"

Wording is important

(waver   to sway   quaver   wave)

Love descends for literal "Hell & back" theatrics

He wants to say desks and whisks
  we are laughing at the glass
table   that language isn't   asks

how the tongue makes hiss with a clatter
of consonant spits   Who are we
to make these noises   to heed

I do he does too   We are silly
poets   a little drunk   The night is
almost over   The night won't be
over until you fall asleep   Silly

Would you like a K sandwich?

We wisely keep these thoughts
to ourselves

INDEX FINGER

skateboard turning
water drips red
sun spanning art
big grew huge

grew green break

fall   *run white*

moving was blood
break small
shoes fall   walk
blue big big
cross pencil
dream moon
hymns exercise

[LOVE IS A PURPLE ANGEL]

Love is a purple angel
half mermaid   s shaped
with a strong hip
Arms say danger: caresses
weakness on the back
of the beaked man-duck
Love has carved the back ground bare
the bat wing strut across the dome
held backs of arm wings
Heart: very skinny

FUNK ENTERS ENGLISH BY 1625

What neural net quirking
needing land and greed to feed me and raw
materials   rivulets to center (little beads)
It's easier than you think
to chop off parts and juggle them

Now notice those dinosaurs on fire
thousands of them
so that the Harley says "potato, potato, potato"

[CROWS AND GRACKLES   GRACKLES]

Crows and grackles   grackles
in the sycamore   food cruising
I'm broke and the sauce burns
I sprinkle ashes in the flowerbed
I kiss your cat

It doesn't matter that fate can't rain
and write flower again
                    Want me a handsome bird
          black toenails that curve
West of Sunny's Wigs
                  the goddess Gaia shaking her dirty hair

[PRETTY HEADDRESS ON KIDUMIEL]

Pretty headdress on Kidumiel
Kick the angel in the air
Kick and beat the brilliant air
Adorn your loud voice

Hurt my broken grinding kiss
Keep your pretty headdress house
I love you, afraid mother
Pure angel Lameck leave me

infant kisses on my T-shirt
Let me bleed fat and big
Slide alongside my boat
to mix my years with serpent tears

[BECAUSE X MARKS THE SPOT]

Because x marks the spot
Because you need popsicle sticks and yarn
to make a god's eye
Because the devil's in the keyhole
Clover leaf me some luck
O smile
My Luden's cough drop sunrise
High-rises divide the sky
Looping you look surprised at the joke
A peace sign
A secret boxy middle

WISH

Good morning it is
still morning   fog lifts to bright
grey laundry sky
soaked through sun   knowing
or to name narrows some
sense in me   wishing fish
would swim through air   multicolored
(orange   white   red)   going somewhere

[FALL IN LOVE IN LUNA]

Fall in love in Luna
County   listen for the fiddle

Breakfast!

                    Handbones cut his hair
Sit outside
                        long in the somber
red of umbra: lunar eclipse
September 26, 1996
Figure eight of my dreams
          Egg in the hole

[GROW BABY GROW A BRAIN WITH CURLY]

Grow baby   grow a brain with curly
hair   blow a leaf   a leaf
shaped love   hold the swirling
life-lasso   draw pretty bubbles baby
(soft rabbit)   the center is
light green   the tender part
is the newest part

[LET ME BE A MEANINGFUL SOUL]

Let me be a meaningful soul
roll of what colored wheat grass
the long line of sky

        You sip   say it's your crazy
                   straw say it's you're crazy
                   as you bicycle your soul
                   with beauty in your basket

I am full of today
                          with my sky blue
nail polish

DEAR DEATH

A simple quibble—what is it that you prize? Pride?
Your winsome vibe aside—we sniff hard at the ruse
of the mondo-young. Whip the moon to a nub
and we would have you new. Human remains
ruined, and I am, wishing for a rune-tattoo to follow.

[SHY MOUTH NOT THE VALUE OF IT (LIPS)]

Shy mouth   not the value of it (lips)
be happy   zoom like this
curious willow I saw
O self cheer   a valley
O joy's selfish traveling

RED JUICE

UP NURSING

Up nursing   then make tea

The word war is far

"Furry,"

says my boy   about the cat

I think anthrax

& small pox vax

Pour hot water on dried nettles

Filter more water for the kettle

Why try

to revive the lyric

THE EARTH IS IN ME

The Earth is in me I'm old
and clay nameless
"grass" with tiny yellow flowers

More mucus this morning to feed warm sperm

The Earth is capable and heals you
You have friends among the weeds
Reddish "sugar ants" next to the mugwort

I had this idea stubbornly
Dog still barking

Write something "new" about the national tragedy

"BY GOODS WE DESTROY GOOD"

what is good   how
is it clear of ruin
what is at the other end
—C. Olson, c. 1952

The possum haw hasn't berried
It is good but no good   twiggy
bent limbs   greening

He came to the door
and asked for money
"I'm stoned," he said (cracked)
and also something sad
in his face about his family
We gave him $10

The "twin of totality"
that writes the poem
The twins Jennie lost
in a swirl of tears and blood
Angelica root   Charcoalized ginger
Infusions for building back the blood

Worried about the work horse
drawing the open carriage
and breathing car fumes

Now alive life   What good
is my worry
cutesy in drawstring pants
pom pom hat

        O I could scream
and scare the baby   and move roughly
Roughly move him   And would you

like some food/to nurse/ a book?
Rumpus   tickle   new little boots

JOURNEY WITH INVESTIGATIVE BEES

for Tom and Philip

I could click the Earth
with my finger   spin
to continents   holding a cardboard box
on my head

              I was trying it out
It was an invention

Buzz over sky curves and the blue
blaze of watery Earth

The black void sucked
The box frayed

"Ranging apart in the phenomenal world" (Tom Clark)

Danger: *dangiere*: dominion

THE UNKNOWN WOMAN

The unknown woman = the distant lover
in the dream needing poetry rules

It's a competition for daughter-in-laws
where blonde always wins
as does Oklahoma

(This means I'm ovulating)

"Thee which is vast the lower regions of Chaos"

I hang on the horn of the moon nibble

The old lover has a receding chin & tartered teeth
so I only "half-heartedly" compete for attention

Where you = me
and the house groans with AC

Oil smeared on limbs

I give birth with ease
a "doubled personality"

YESTERDAY

Yesterday in the periwinkle house
the lake was skinned   Membranes
pushed into the dream of the world
A child   the earth   a fetter   an oar

The stones are porous and fit into small hands
We arrange them on gold lacquered coasters
I crack the eggs and fry potatoes

"The muse with cookies"

Rushing   the semen climbs
A mucus bridge-way   riding thunder
or pumpkins   that plumping

Avoid fortified wine and strong drink
said the angel   She tends
symbolic birthing   stovetop   cooking sauce

WORE A HEMP HAT

Wore a hemp hat   ate grapes
A list of future baby names:
Waylon   *Angelica*   *Martin*   *Lucia*
Rhymed some words & read a poem
Still damp   (the laundry)   Come on sun
Swished the toilets and watered plants
By March I'll have gained 2 pounds
in uterine muscle   Ate gross cinnamon bun

WOMEN WITH SHARP NOSES

Women with sharp noses and underdeveloped
third portions of their faces
Skin wings spread wide   scary for their snake hair
and fingers loosely clutching daggers
My hands cover my ears

The rocky soil holds no visible life
I wear my favorite lace-up knee boots
It's the anxiety of a terrible future
where we might have to move our debt
to Vancouver or Morocco somewhere
with Universal Health Care   food
straight from growers   no stickers
on my apples   otherwise known as
how can we live on one state employee pension

They float in a grey cloud   my mother
in the dream   slurring and taking
off her shoes   I can't feel the
baby yet   how can you be
in love with the baby

YOU SAY THE LAND

You say the land
itself articulates

Form presses out and in

How to explain winter   and sleigh rides
with our latitude
& our pickup trucks

Waxed mustaches in mesquite thickets
Willful women in West Texas

I want a large ass
like the large-assed women
the ancients drew
on certain cave walls in the Pyrenees

What if the spine of the land is a monster
cf. our "blow out" on I-35

Pulled off onto the shoulder:
rush of cars   *monstrous*
fouled air   spewing

This week   gunmen steal "The Scream"
(painted on cardboard)
bits of frame found in the street

And I do think it's true that men stole
the magical instruments of women

& we were too busy
with ordinary life
to worry about this

A LILY MOTHER

A lily mother　　　gaping is a chasm
no that's chaos　　　a swirl hole
with a poke staff　　　　keeping track of the sky

When talk is dirty and we do it

I am vine-like with small white flowers
I'm eating breast milk (goat cheese)　Leaves
and fruit hang down

I FOUND HIM BENEATH A TREE

Unease comes and plucks the babe
the tree weeps   languid   long leaves
like her hair is long   She lifts the baby
by the head   from the puckering ground

Last night the room was vast and white
he played handball   it was a theater
with his small sad apartment out of sight   (shabby)
and the white white room looked like purgatory

"He struggles into life"   and so Earth burps
as wasting disease takes Michigan deer
Hooves wander with swollen deer brains   Congress
alarmed   kills and kills   The plucked babe sneezes

SPRING SONNET

Purple ground cover with pink flowers spring
hopeful   Bring soil to the round row of peas
(no blooms)   Nothing and I mean nothing
beyond the fence   (OK, weeds)   and I'm nearing
the ninth month and move around this belly
in honor of Demeter and her poppies
"Ordinary people do most of the living
and dying around here"   The traffic glides
Maybe the grackles feasted on the seeds
under the desert willow you planted
I get weepy reading Dorn's graveyard poem
The grey cat picks her way across goose grass

EURASIACAN

No mother in body no
body when on the phone
meatballs simmering in sauce

Maybe my baby
whitens me
Turtles and blue eyes

"Pet" turtles discard
in the pond
crusty deformed shells

Ground deer
meatballs mixed
in my mutt hands

Mã = horse
Ma. = rice seedling
Ma? = graveyard
Má = mother

My boy walks
arms out pointing
at the window

Yes you saw a lizard
there once   Yes you rode
a dolphin   and a seal

RONALD McDONALD

Ronald McDonald as a "spokesperson"
makes my 3 faces scream   hair turn flame-like
A clown with large denominations
super super white face

Trickle down on me

Hang a giant stars-and-stripes flag
Make it a backdrop   Throw question marks in the air
Stars seen from the "correctional facility" that means
I have 6 eyes and nostrils

The news pictures the beheaded defense contractor
wearing a cowboy hat   6 eggs fell today
(toddler accident)

          Our neighbor says he's leaving
for Fairfield   staying with family
"They like to barbecue"

Focus on the good parts
for "positive thinking"

Neighborhood statuary:
3 frogs in the "see no evil" etc. joke

THE SECRECY OF ARMS AT DAWN

I sleep and wake   baby at the breast
Announce   "I am a weaver"   fold
laundry

The smell of lively flowers

I spun the baby out of you and me
"energy buttons"

I am she who unknots the cord
and lashes us   boatless

Poisonous caterpillar alternating yellow and black stripes
likewise red and black   on backs of certain snakes

Red seizes me   toes blood crimson

Empty my womb   a clotty summary
of wax wax wax   now wane and water
the plants with bloody water
water & blood   a cupful
a latex-y cup   to catch the monthly spill

"Does the moon
menstruate?"

Redundant redundant
question question

IF I CAN'T HAVE ANOTHER BABY

If I can't have another baby   I'll bake
midnight cookies   a little nut cookie

Forming something out of nothing

or   more precisely   a more complex something
from a simpler something

"The rising flood is the begetter of gods"

I drink from a cup and so draw my omens

The man said, "We could never do that . . ."
motioning towards my toddler-infant "balancing act"

BLACKBERRIES

Blackberries deep black from the farm stand
little seeds to grind dead & alive & ripe

Spirits taught me to write
Countless spirits writing this

Red juice I threw the book down
Furious!
Poetry you're a ripening disease

Grind write the dead

THE GODDESS GAVE ME ROSES

The goddess gave me roses several
loose blooms the way my cervix flowered
and let the baby out

We drink tea
a rose tied to her waist the rose
is a baby and flames regard
the cracked pottery where women's things
are is culture domestic

Dale says according to Sauer
that men only later and then "reluctantly"
took up domestic ways weaving
clay works the cooking arts language

Women as masters & teachers

The goddess came as a stinkbug
on the edge of her tea cup
6 black legs edged in dusty red
Back shaped like a shield
with a faint x topped by a y

Grackles eat the cat food

LACY LIGHT

for D., K. and Way

Lacy light through new curtains
          curtains Mary made

and seem recent like lamp oil
burning on my shoulder

It's chaos & love   Big
                    Old

Being literal about banjos
stuck to kneecaps

Crack up   say mangos

O Susannah   o don't you cry

It's a mango on my knee

Up Nursing: Nettles are used as a liver and blood tonic and support the endocrine system, cleansing and nourishing the glands. It is high in minerals, especially iron and calcium, and many vitamins. To make an infusion, put a handful of dried nettles in a wide-mouth jar and add just-boiled filtered water. Cover and steep for 4 hours or overnight; strain and drink.

The Earth Is in Me: Using the Fertility Awareness Method or FAM (not to be confused with the Rhythm Method) women track changes in cervical mucus as a means of conceiving or preventing pregnancy, thereby avoiding synthetic hormones, barrier methods that rely on petro-chemicals, or surgery.

"By Goods We Destroy Good": title is an old Anglo Saxon saying, taken, along with the epigraph, from an essay by Charles Olson reprinted in *Apex of the M*.

Journey with Investigative Bees takes its title from a line drawing by Philip Trussell. The penultimate and final lines were drawn from notes taken during Tom Clark's class on the Renaissance poet Sir Thomas Wyatt.

The Unknown Woman: the italicized words were drawn from Carl Jung's *Memories, Dreams, and Reflections*.

Yesterday was written on the occasion of the homebirth of

Jasper, son to next-door neighbors Dana and Diana, July 4, 2003.

You Say the Land: According to Gimbutas in *The Language of the Goddess* "the exaggerated buttocks are a metaphor for the double egg or pregnant belly: intensified fertility . . . The symbolisms expressed reverence for supernatural potency, expressed by the doubling device, the 'power of two.'" Also references *The Wise Wound* by Shuttle and Redgrove.

A Lily Mother: St. Bridget's Day 2003. Bridget is a triple goddess ruling fire, healing waters, the well, fertility, divination, smithcraft, poetry.

Spring Sonnet quotes George Bailey from *It's a Wonderful Life* and refers to the poem "The Air of June Sings" by Edward Dorn.

Ronald McDonald: "With a record-setting 2 million people now locked up in American jails and prisons, the United States has . . . a higher percentage of its citizens behind bars than any other country." (*Baltimore Sun*, June 1, 2003). According to the Bureau of Justice Statistics, the U.S. rate is now 707 prisoners per 100,000 residents, or about 2.2 million incarcerated (International Centre for Prison Studies, May 2014).

Unhemmed Latitude: quote from *The Wise Wound* by Shuttle and Redgrove.

If I Can't Have Another Baby: italicized words were drawn from Carl Jung's *Memories, Dreams, and Reflections*.

Blackberries: written under the influence of Boggy Creek Farm blackberries, in response to a volume of *Best American Poetry* and after Wm. Shakespeare's Sonnet 86:

> Was it the proud full sail of his great verse,
> Bound for the prize of all too precious you,
> That did my ripe thoughts in my brain inhearse,
> Making their tomb the womb wherein they grew?
> Was it his spirit, by spirits taught to write
> Above a mortal pitch, that struck me dead?
> No, neither he, nor his compeers by night
> Giving him aid, my verse astonished.
> He, nor that affable familiar ghost
> Which nightly gulls him with intelligence
> As victors of my silence cannot boast;
> I was not sick of any fear from thence:
> But when your countenance fill'd up his line,
> Then lack'd I matter; that enfeebled mine.

The Goddess Gave Me Roses: St. Bridget's Day 2004—Candlemas, also known as Imbolc "in the belly of the mother."

Lacy Light: "lamp oil" references the story of Eros and Psyche.

HECATE LOCHIA

SOME THINGS

Some things are subordinate to other things
in the order of things

Fish wriggle in water
Crows on sky tethers winging
and eating roadkill

It's difficult after all
to tell where one ends and another begins

Environments collapse how can I
have another baby There being
too much human pee and not enough energy

ADD SOME BLUE

Add some blue to it
                    your eyes that can't see yet
add some blue there   Texas
a big car-fever as my blue
car fades   paint fades in the sun

Texas says "we're friendly"
It's midday and we hear cars
adding some blue
Make it a blue
highway to drive home
to the world's end

Blue can spell your name   I don't
know that yet either   wrapped up
in the snake's coil   and wipe my hands

You have all the blue a little bit of
blue   like a blue turtle
encased in red-blue   blue-red
the throbbing vein

Who will I be now
going through the blue door
that is going through me

I need you descending
and giving breath
I think I'm writing
this blue to get to you

THINKING OF BERNADETTE

Thinking of Bernadette   trying to live without
money   Having written three checks today
(food)   I'd rather trade but make no
"valuable" goods   There is no gold standard
as the value of money and Boggy Creek go
winding
          Regulation authorities come
into being   Laugh tracks behind
the simplest things like 2 men speaking
with boing-ing sound effects (radio)   Ate
ginger miso with buckwheat noodles bought
with inconvertible money   (Where *are* my metals?)
and backed by—   as the French call it
liberating power

BLUE NORTHER

"Blue Norther" and the day of the Epiphany

Draw mustaches on the King's
portrait   draw on yourself with a burnt cork

Find a bean baby in the cake

The bonfire is for fooling
King Herod (wink wink)
Read: old Saturnalia
and the even older she-sun celebration

The unconquerable sun

Added currants and coconut
to the sweet rice recipe
one crushed clove
and maple syrup for the *dulce*

Among the ancients we find
admonitions against red food
            No red food
on certain festival days

This might be
fear of birth-blood
fear of moon-blood   (monthly blood)

Fear of the female principal

“I eat you   You eat me”

PUTT PUTT THE CAR

After you rescue all the baby animals
the cars can visit them   driving into
the zoo saying "Yay"
                    But then
the game ends   before the cars can enjoy
the families inside their enclosures

BIRTHDAY POEM

Swimming in a sea of English —***Kerouac***

It's my birthday and throw myself
a party Hard to be born live variously
and have a job Be grateful
for the job heat in winter 9 AM
and 3 I love you's Wipe poop

It's game day on TV Sunday
"Play-offs"
War language and dancing butts
like that one in tight play-off pants

I disappear I disappear drink beer
Eating is dying like a sandwich
Enjoy your sandwiches

POST HURRICANE IKE
ALMOST EQUINOX

Stained by blood

blood stains

on the bedsheets

your palm with jizz & blood

Heavenly

maps swirl Torpor for air

We a throbbing ear

The buzzing “juh” is not symbolized:

Measure

Pleasure

Leisure

Fissure

Moist wind blew the door open

WE ARE FREE TO EAT

We are free to eat and love
We spray on poison   ants bite me
I am writing towards the things-in-three rule

If you are in my poem   driving
a purple pickup   with a blinker on
"Play the music loud"
Make it make-out music
Fuck-me music
The Al Green song I like to strip to

The ground is cracked from lack of rain
We're in the shade   writing
There are rose thorns and the huge legume family

I'm on the verge of swimming

  The sky is a time-arch   with feeling

Various shreds on the ground:
        red foil
        old grey mulch
        dried bee belly

GOD

God hates you
the sign says
            Crocus dark

as art hides in the reaching
Me loud & I spill my cups

The deity flees

My bleeding bedding

IRIS AGAIN

I could have wings and stand
alongside the other gods but
not in my own right
          Spilling it
and going back and forth

                    My hair is so frizzly
crazy wires   humid air

Rainbows are really circles?

Bearded flowers   purple
with yellow tongue-y centers
          The green green hills are mellow
rounded like breasts   I guess

I just keep POURING and POURING

          What a dumb job   I remind you
to flow-on because getting stuck

I get stuck and have to experiment like this
Prism-ing light and a flowy gown

Is it always about circles?

I circle you   You ghost me
and become a ghost   finally

DUST

And it all may evaporate at once
Brittle notes from poetry

Food
          buy three cans of soup a day
because it doesn't require water

This is a colorful madness

We need a tarp   a magnifying glass
matches

I'M IN VERY

I'm in very trouble
spirally sun   contact slides
Am watched by your I
Not I   but a girl
and I can whirl her into me
until she is my face
            not crouched next to shoulders

The cardinals birdie birdie birdie

More droppings   seed riot
Beautific fluff and lopping
Big biceps from lifting children

There's that sun again

THE SIZE

The size is all wrong but the genetics
is 27%   Loiters for miles
and I'm done with cigarettes
excepting the mother-shame
            You
like a writing table
                                    Me writing
limply   Butt up against the target

My arms alarm and the blood
bites back

            Hang a pirate flag
You who are white and male
            or go
"find your voice in the dark"

WATER THAT FALLS FROM THE SKY

Move like your favorite animal
and experiment

          Space is huge
without talking   and tiny things

Seeds point up completely new

We make stick-on eyes
for the furniture in the house

Today we "Invent our own
Celebration"

                    And squish
a giant cockroach in front of guests

Tet 2006, the Year of the Dog

PURPLE VOMIT

or what was said on Tuesday
when I made goat cheese

and I'm sweeping
goat cheese   puffed rice   hair

"Mercury dwells in matter
            more especially the bit
of original chaos   hidden in creation"

I keep wanting to make
"clean food" except for today
Sunday which is garlic
sundried tomatoes   olive oil

Mercury is the figure
of the poet   always moving very quickly

and teasing you with absurd knock knock jokes

Curved horns on the symbol for woman

"It has been repeatedly stated
that the soul is a sphere"

I whirl around and around
            on the potter's ground
and part of the back fence fell down

LONG LIGHT

Long light   Super Bowl Sunday 2006
"Do" to escape from the present
lying on a recycled-plastic outdoor-carpet
near profuse clover and the water meter

In the dream Heather
marries a heart surgeon in heaven

We need to empty the ash from our chiminea

Peely bark on the sycamore tree   waxing
gibbous moon

There are rhetorical happenings (written directly
onto a flower)

Can love
everyone?

I DISGORGE THE VEGETATION

I disgorge the vegetation
Face of leaves: live vine
acanthus   oak

See Sheila-na-gig: I jack off like that
God in the whizzing wind

Foliate face
          I sneeze summer vines
as my words are leaves

Jack in the Green

TREMENDOUS

"Tremendous active
critical energy and weight"

Water is so fucking heavy
all those cubic feet

Watery Binah
The Great Mother

"The redeeming belly which kills"

PROP

And his key had a bike tool it was multi-tooled
which will be handy when camping or
for the inevitable fleeing from marauding suburban
desperation Crops in the front yard
next to the driveway

We have a map of San Francisco
showing which streets will be
underwater

And shadowy shapes visuals
that indicate the former forms of ice-cap glaciers

A prop to present to the President

ANOTHER STABBING BOLDFACE

While I wait, a shining beige/brown chevron
clothes-moth settles on the bedspread —***Philip Whalen***

Great tailed grackle
          often in thousands

Ranging   I have the head
and hands of an insect

whether "Lady Bee" or
"Lady Butterfly"
          Wings like a double-axe

The snakes crawl
          The beasts howl   (dogs)

Antennae like bull's horns

"Lady of the Wild Things"

ORANGEY

Orangey thieves   The thatch
of days   Every day is
ordinary with fish-sticks   Picking
skull-crap from our 4 year old's
head
        Nicely we crud   overlay
Our bed is encumbered
        We
strip at night and the light
is on   The pretty lanterns
strung on the dirty porch
or you can see me now   You
who are snappy and I'm
there happy to turn into you

DRIPPY

Drippy   what does this say
    about my emotional state

Cry at the joke about K-mart
Cry at the photo of the woman crying
(baby born dead   held in her arms)

Life penetrates life   I am free-form today
    fermenting a loaf of bread

The oven is warm
    I need to bake a chicken
        Raining again

A CRIME PENDULANT

And the hamster couldn't fly it would slam
on the concrete Grey like the weather of today
heading to "Leap Day" Sleeping in late because your
lover lets you in Don't fuck it up freely

If I could spill my blood red or marshal a blue
a blue ribbon building a buttress of blue
and squiggles
I would

NO SLEEP

No sleep   no sleep escape
Milk raining down
turning lilies white

Mena presided over moon-blood
Her offerings: young puppies
that still sucked their mother

Formaldehyde in the sheets
to be wrinkle-free

April 2006   5X the average in tornadoes
and thriving poison ivy

The sky turns green

Old Roger has died and gone to his grave
gone to his grave   gone to his grave
Old Roger has died and gone to his grave
Heigh ho   gone to his grave

"Several ice-sheets in Greenland
have doubled their rate of slide"

My boy blows a plastic whistle (parrot-shaped)
          stamped   Made in China

WRITE FUCKED UP POEMS

Write fucked up poems round or layered
You know cabbaged and I will egg you
Full moon Spring Equinox
just passed and heavy rose blooms
unseasonably cold and record snow

The rose is called "Katy Road"

A fucked poem from the start and the
rattling beak of Road Runner
in the driveway descending cry
of Road Runner
eater of snakes and lizards

Egg in the sky May
a fertile time
Strawberries from CA

In the Magic Kingdom
lies Tomorrow Land
the "first great malls" and
the "worship of vehicles"

Tape a stone over your womb
named *Black Apache Tears*

I'M SORRY FOR YOU SAD MARIGOLDS

I'm sorry for you   sad marigolds   rain pummeled
We have a "perfect" sky now   as cardinals
and mockingbirds become the birds of suburbs

    Jet plane   with cloud backdrop
Paint the house that blue of sky

A comeback *is* possible

That's Sarge's house with bleached mammal bones
and 4 sycamores frame the curb-view

Zack sits on the storm drain by the dying elm

"What are you doing today?"
    "Writing poems."   "Right now?"

Old style pop-tops   embedded in the asphalt

9 FLAT FLIES IN THE HOUSE

it's one huge reckless orchestra —***Eileen Myles***

Squirrel scolding and grackles
Really what could the upset be
Christine's stomach growls   "Excuse me"
Phone rings   work   must
replace the employee
you no longer want and now hates you

Face the purple flowers
in the flower food water
Texas-grown   sucking stems
named *Anemone*

Hating my needing to be loved

Dear Texas   here I am
near your "heart"   and the "Value Sky Park"
Jumping spider on the kitchen counter

"I don't know what I'm learning"

"That's the point"

ALL THE FAILED

All the failed poems   grocery
receipt dropping to the floor

The water-stressed
landscape

Mammals seek moist buds
Eat the rockrose

We eat   we have to
eat   munch
And have a caterpillar
lunch?

Squeeze out the innards
to avoid irritant hairy outards

BUTTERFLIES, BREASTMILK, CHINESE JADE, CONTINUOUS PRESENT, & MOTORCYCLES

for my Mother and after B. Mayer

Bought a butterfly wheel for matching
butterflies to younger version
of butterflies (grub) and favorite food

Spin the wheel to identify
even when things are messy
like women's things
blood all the time   blood rites
like breastmilk

Harleys drive past for a Bike Rally downtown

Language is a book conscious of the eating
world   the breathing world   the alien
self and her lover/son

I was drawn to the green jade   smooth
like the circle you wore clicking
against counters   steering wheels
Taken off later with much effort and butter

The continuous present streams by
          We step in it

My "I" is too cluttered with paper
Mail everyday much of it "junk mail"
You have to tear it in half
and sidewalk chalk vivid colors

The bikers wear leather it's better for riding
Looks good usually tight and smells like skin & chemicals

I like seeing useful breasts Babies
eating even older babies and toddlers
Mothers talking and showing breast skin
It's food I'm making milk right now

Drove our car past motorcycles to Kim's farm for chickens

You rode motorcycles "stunt style"
pedal pushers long hair
gossip of the obsessed lovers
The religious student who followed you as the circus moved
from his town meeting his parents

You are one quarter Cambodian that makes me
what percentage Cambodian
Is the Cham tribe
in my blood? Stone carvings
with sexy bosoms on their temples

The rainforest reclaims them

Yellow Butterfly you say
is your name   Diep   means Yellow Butterfly
Sexy starlet looks   Silver Snake woman
like my oldest son   also a Silver Snake

          More Harleys
pass by   like the continuous present
          Wake up the baby

STRANGELY TOUCHED

Strangely touched that Vili and Mary Kay tied the knot
8 AM rain   now hot hot   Memorial Day
And last night's dream with drowning
kittens in the bloody toilet bowl
            more moon-mess in the tub
& I laugh even when my father stops
and says, "hi"

10 AM whacked the wool bed pad
on the line with a long rod and smote
dust mites
            Also carried wash and 2 kids
in a plastic basket

The phone rings
  "It's me" "I love you"

I STOLE THAT

I stole that laughing Buddha
statuette

Maybe have to steal things
like possum
no
goody-goody Apollo

BIG HEART SMALL HEART

Growing a heart   another heart
A deep cavity in the shape of an X

The eyes are hollow or covered
          Good fix   God   Bad boy
Percale sheets and cooking spray

What isn't an historic moment
crossing it out
                    bundled

War–Mouth–Eyes
(Shiva/Horus)

          The will to live/die
is not incompatible

I LIKE BEING LUCKY

Stupid in-box
Time a shimmery
autumn backdrop

Long precise shadows I clutch
a powder-blue pillbox purse
and brooding eyebrows

and stepping on the undead
the suburb-surviving zombies

I spear the bloody head onto the fence post

Trumpet
The Flood Next Time

ODE

We ate outside   you could smell the ocean
and petrol   Seagulls scream
look for pieces for food or what have you

Go look for pieces   the lost
body   Bury that piece   Clams
and their rich stomachs
at Little Neck

What kind of ode is this?

"She moulded human images
out of wax and spices"

We eat pretend desserts
normally chocolate
but sometimes pickle cake

NEEDING

for D.

Needing to get to you
China   on a "monkey bridge"
(wearing shoes)   an airport dream
and why do I insist on being angry
when I merely mean to be
insistent
Saturday night
and your belly with gas

We're standing on the rim
of a popular vista   10 years ago
Grand Canyon Arizona
shabby grad school clothes   more fat
in our faces   arms in symmetry angled to each side

Maybe the afterworld will be sexy

I'm attached to the jasmine vine growing
on the porch even though
it might bring roaches into the house

o Passage

(went inside to finish the poem)

Another year of air
Storm leaves turning in the morning

GREAT MOTHER OF THE GODS

Cybele   among many
other names
Her sacred symbol: a small
meteoric stone (black)

All-begetter
All-nourisher
The Mother of the Blest

Great Nature Goddess:
Mountain Mother
Great Mother of the Gods
Mother of all Gods and all Men [sic]

also as Ma or Ammas

Caves = Cybele

(hair fragrant with ointment)

Niobe of Mt. Sipylus
is really the Mother

She is generally pictured with 2 lions
under her arms

I CAN EXTRACT MYSELF / FROM THAT EMOTION

title and poem after Alice Notley

Blonde   my sister's boyfriend
Rich   I think fortune-tellers
play tricks: my sister foretold
"You will be rich. Very Rich."

In the morning
dream   he is blonde
and tan and working on a "dude ranch"
which reminds me
to email my sister: no visit home
this week

Heather is teaching like she always did
Circles projected onto air showing articles
of clothing and esoteric womanly art-
secrets   a circle skirt   chunky beads
(very important)
Heather with a weak face for a moment
I'm not sure what I'm learning
"That's the point"

Once with Robin she journeyed
Why “journeyed”?   Okay her
spirit moved through lifetimes until she was
a man spinning spinning spinning
her bride in her arms   Death by drowning

What about the water
table and navy poly smocks?

Life life love   Live

THE SUN PERSON

The sun person breastfeeding the sun
infant
 Angry territory noise
passing through serene sun goddess ear space
and it might be Australia covering her crotch

I could sit on the edge
of fields nurse and rest

My boy holding up fruit
and a book at my feet
sheaves of wheat in place of hair

And nursing on the other side now
comfortable next to crops
a child at my elbow

"No mystery was ever celebrated without dancing"

They went to the shore
and purified with sea-
water and probably
a sprinkling of pig's blood

The corn spirit
is a pig
        A sow & her rows of milky teats

HORSE HERB

Horse herb legs around
                                        and a fungus
rots the remains of elm root

Our native meadow "lost
to the plow"   You devour
habitat   are the brown-
headed cow bird

Heather wants bracted-twisted flowers
wants me to twist T shirts
and dip them into dye

                          Instead
I smear the stove with avocado

Now Lady Elms arrives
in the kitchen   long blonde hair
lean body   leaves
She shows me a profile and a letter

Everyone is a sexual being

SEAGULLS

to Poets

Seagulls
Wrap food around a stone
Throw it
Bird crashes   dispatch
Eat it

UGLY POEM

Can go spiral or back & forth
with weather fronts   "in between" weather
Humid   Weird bird calls at dusk

The raucous perches and sunsets pretty
with bird shit   Patio furniture
with bird art

    "Chop Chop
"   is the name we give the neighbor
The man who lost his legs and lives
        across the street

I'M DRIVING

I'm driving from the back seat
have to dive over the front seat
to get to the brakes and there's glass
on the floor from my freak-out fury

Attach an email printout to your naked hip
to show how pissed-off you are

We stayed at a farm called North Farm
You can't name it "Dolittle"
after the farm-to-market road

Drought may be "broken"
by El Niño rain
cold front
contrails
bubbly birthday wine

Why did you   no don't say it

"Catastrophic global disruptions"
predicted by 2100

SEEDS STUCK IN GROUND

Seeds stuck in ground
The child sprinkles seeds all around

Borage for my milk
Calendula for baby
skin

                    Pale green sprouts
bring up seed hulls
by dirty feet

People began as wood   dough   dirt
cooked in salty water

"What is today's number?"

The last day of school
and a black hook scoops the sun

Items found in city tap water:

Flouride

Chlorine

Birth control pill hormones

Antibiotics

STRUT

Chicken violence like "bucket of chicken"   Headless
chicken at Ma's farm

running 'til its life runs out   There's nowhere to go
from here but gone

        Vibrate   Raise your hand
in a fist   Fetal chicks in pregnancy
Fetal chicks for bone strength

—triangles—   —triangles—   —triangles—

Woman-shaped brown
                anchored & naked & issuing

I have something to tell you   My wavy arms
   outstretched
Listen to the frond shapes

The stages of baby are

(My heart outside my body   in my arms)

Dance with your limbs askew
        Y shaped

I SAID APPREHEND TO SEIZE

Eve's necklace after the legume
seed-pod   black and segmented
Chunky black beads
And "in the madness of spring": pink
Flowers drooping in clusters

Burn up thy thought

Star
The mother
Aquarius   (window)

PUSA

Old English *pusa* "bag"
Something soft and cuddly

What a beautiful pussy you are   you are   you are

"Love the world   stay inside it"

My own private pussy   and the feminist claims I make
that I pour a glass of wine for
and cultivate   growing a child

2 parabolic jaws
to eat fruit-flavored gummy teeth   Dracula style

Of Mona Lisa's smile
emotion recognition programs determine
83% happy   9% disgusted   6% fearful   2% angry

THE BALLERINA IN A MUSIC BOX

The ballerina in a music box and flowery
pink mesh thongs   Horsey good looks

Paint this in 5 colors
My back chilled by north wind
                    gap in my clothes

Grackles in the hackberry   A stain

I've always enjoyed monster movies

Now you can eat cloned livestock

WASHINGTON

Washington (George) is not in
this poem   powdered wig powdery
and anyway who chops down a fruit
tree   (idiots)
                              My sense of
history lies   We buy things
::::chicken wings::::::butter:::::

Yesterday Dave took away
my office   my boss   Saturday

FEBRUARY 2, 2007

Hairy she's wild
with a Chinese Lantern face
Frizzley muhly for hair

She should be darker she eases
Greenland ice sheets
Pissed off
Why she would say "Fuck Hecate"

Crooked bayberry candle
(I almost wrote baby berry)

Lashed with jasmine

15 degrees Aquarius and thus
confused brilliant cunning

YOU CAN RIDE

You can ride outside the plane but it's scary
clutching your backpack   Ride
on the wing   all the way to Boulder
and then look for your missing satchel for hours
in the airport

Transitions and the part of yourself
that hates
you   the other person
in the shape of the sweeper

Catch pasty butterflies for your critter cage

We've won the climate change bonanza
Mild summer   lush lush gardens

For the first time in a century
the Chinese statue above the dammed lake
can churn its legs in the water
Male statue of a man
        Green legs churning

SHORT

Short like Prince   the man does a foolish dance
Pants on backwards

A white man   an owner
    of opinions and properties

He didn't earn the opinions
He made them in his factory

NO ONE WANTS

No one wants to remove
our poison ivy   not even for money

I drink out of a jar
"Fermentation is permaculture"
and drive too much—everywhere

"There *is* no there there"

Driving a hole
in the ozone layer

Grey transformer box
hulks in the backyard
and we have the 60th anniversary
of the bombing of Hiroshima

White refrigerator on
all day

MOUNTAIN GORILLAS

Mountain gorillas   one named "Future"
Newborn naming ceremony
Name her Future

Summer 2007   Mountain gorillas are 700
On Monday   Hollywood celebrity names one
Future   A metallic gorilla taste in my mouth
getting out of the car
                  $85.73 goods
      Food and general wares
No gorilla wine named Guture   A metallic
gallbladder taste and liver and spleen
and gorilla energy in the right shin

Survival energy   shoulder blade
an effective saw shape
leaving gorilla shaped hole

Her face was rough   Rock face or porous
Like a pumice stone   Skin pores enlarged
with age
      That's Virgo the magma gorilla
The mama gorilla
Waking up the earth gorilla   mountain gorilla earth

I COULD SCREAM

I could scream outside of Mi Madres'
Cantina slinky
and in a sophisticated rage
make "serious poetry" like scrambled eggs

The in-between parts move
Rare shadows on my cheeks
"Spirits of love" feed me summer
I wrote: "my heart speaks for shadows"
in my notebook

Cut your hair
"I dig you"

Today winks with fullness
sharpened
Sharp New

"Poesia Seriosa":

Kick your sleep
Unwind on a lap
Dimmer switch
Dinner and a hand

In mystery rites there are things
which “could not be said”
only acted out

THIS COLLAPSE

"This collapse in housing
is sucking all borrowing"
          and the wind was blowing
just right   I could listen
to that weather song   Kiss
a bomb tattoo   and pint night

Forget it

          Blame ordinary
maudlin beasties   Kisses
more of them   primary
and what would you like
in a leather jacket   Colder
wind   Kiss it
now

LIVING

Living in the dream under a US regime
that legalized and actively encouraged
random racism
          I was the outspoken
sister   Defiant and scared
in the parking garage
at the racist aggro frat boy

How to make dream-jelly when birds
love them   We name birds

                    Kingfisher
all trilly
          a beefy kind of bird

"Life eats life"   Here's a fig

Wheeling black vultures   collect now in the elm
frosted black wings

My 3-faced goddess nests in the roots
a fruit for child birth

(I wrote child bird originally)

and think
he will go far   being male & white-looking & attractive

Gather leaves and dry them   Sew them
with reed string
                    for to make me a book

A story within a story

   Tree-roots mirror branches   or veins
     like a placenta

Rowan's bitter berries sweeten after frost

CUPID RIDES

Cupid rides a goddam dolphin
at the hand of Venus
                Clever eyes
we'd be surprised to see
& then bathe by the sea

THE STARBUCKS MERMAID

The Starbucks mermaid logo
has lost her nipples

I coffee you a bit
fiery with my purple tongue
& random sadness

Gasoline @ $65 dollars a barrel
(13 August 2005)

You can plug your phone
into the Tibetan bowl bell (on sale)
for a more pleasing tone

We put the poopy blocks
outside   and then it rained

MEDINA APPLES

Medina apples ripen and arrive
this week   more flies   rain
more complaining and mud
in the house

            I might literally shut down
like a bug   little legs
curled in the air

            US houses
have little relation to the outside
and nowhere
for walkers to walk

Now it's August
AC: in
Hot: out

            Also headlines
of brain dead woman dying
after giving birth
and peaches from "the hill country"

GET DEBT RELIEF

Get debt relief now
Dahlia   crimson with yellow tips

I could eat a poisonous flower
cover eyes with a coin

"Money affects virtually every interaction
we have with other people"

I'm dying   pushing my grey body
toward the make-up counter

UPSIDEDOWN AGAIN

Held by the roots   like the cilantro
beaten in my mortar
Make a chicken marinade and broil
Could pluck feathers after scalding?

O circled fucked-up change

which is the mother of us
and ethics   What of that
Chicken feathers
to grow your organic vegetables

The wild will root it out
The pigs dig them up   your roots
Lovely smiling pig to string up on a pole
Fatten you   o lovely

I am the omnipotent narrator noting
the age-wrinkles around his neck

The play we make in the snow in Colorado
a survivalist trick   A snow-made den
to live in   or wave your umbrella

from your stranded car
at the rescuing helicopter

I can't stomach all these circles
or my head noise
even cartoon songs
from animated Cat in the Hat
in the woods walking the woo woo
labyrinth   (alone)

I have fetal tissue in my brain
literally

and Chinquapin Oak on my placenta in the rain

It hasn't rained like this
since they were born
meaning our boys

A woman is the person
the first person
like a chicken before an egg

TUESDAY

"Here comes the rain"
and I should make pizza
Vivid heirloom tomatoes

Still lunging around with poems

More soldiers dead
in Iraq
and Bush
is the fittest president in history
going for a jog on vacation again
(with cute dogs as pets)

"Better times approach"

CLIMB

Climb through books
Want and what am I
          The park
weirdly spins   The car
parked close by

Rings
weep

We have a clean feeling
Say “no” to emotions
Smear a small red spider
A cleaning fire

BUILDING

"building a metal heart"
Must blue   must blue
on the background of blue
and it blew up literally
Fuse lit blew and the wind blew
under my dress and I was wrong
about the metal propane heaters

Spiderman action figure
on the doorknob
Dirty dirty feet

Tonight is leftovers: beans
kale   chicken

THE PROBLEM

The problem with the lights and the
smell of apples   rotting sliced apples
I put into the lights
cleaning them out
in order to see better   not a good spot
for apples

I talked to the invasive tree
how to replace China Berry   Poison ivy
Running bamboo   humans   Literally
knocking it over   crack the big limb
how to restore   as in the children's book
looking for the ordinary snortle pig
plants   animals and homes equally numbered

Peed in the backyard   long black skirt
to mark this mine
I talked to the tree   pee smell
for raccoons and possum natives

Death is the return to the mother
return to the wet place

Our local creek: Boggy
my fear of it   stagnant smell   trash
and rats   nesting lesser herons   rocks and
bottle tops

Water sample August 4, 2006
North Boggy Creek at Airport Blvd.
Nitrate 2.08   BAD
Phosphate .07   POOR

Sinking   reading of massive phyto-plankton
& algae bloom
Hypoxic zone   Gulf of Mexico dead zone
Sized larger than New Jersey

August Perseids seen
from the stoop

FRAYING

Is that an eye you hide the orange bit
Freak out squiggles over the main part
and shit on the goose grass Blueness
That is the sky dome
Dry cleavers to tincture A tonic
Spongy parts of me Unlikely as it is for me
to love I do

WHAT WAS IN HER ASH-WOOD BOX

There are always centers
and "heavy boundaries"

A pit I can't peel &
you want to keep your ampersands

Could vomit snakes
into a bucket
taking three minutes to find a pen

My front tooth   I offer this dead
tooth   rattle it in a bulbous gourd I grew

The baby figure has three fingers
grain of rice sized

No more babies for me

CHINA PLANS

China plans to paint more mountains green
Green paint the scars   The strip-mining scars

Beautification to make a noun of it

Decorate strip-mining scars
for Olympic tourists
Paint the mountain green

It's a permit
It's permitted
We permit you

Dump 6 million fish into the Yellow River

The Kia car promises "Giddyupness"
to make a noun of it

Blast me into outer space
            Space for more bass notes
in anonymous cars (driving and thumping)

Enormous mouse cars
More Olympic-tourist-sized cars

"If worst comes to worst, the Virgin Moon sounds pretty good. We'll colonize it"

—Sir Richard Branson on Virgin Galactic

MONSTERS IN THE MYTH

Monsters in the myth swallow you
as I was swallowed and disgorged or chopped in two
and you who do not shit the toxic taxoplasma gondii parasite
and thus kill the North American Otter

Slits in the belly
whole and unharmed   human   emerging again

Come the parasite
from run-off water

Rain and tiny ants that invade our kitchen counter
washes eggs from shit into
waterways   ocean   sprayed with full-strength
vinegar

Stars say: time of scales   hated by Dale
equinox move into Libra

The Yoke or Beam of the Balance
All that's left is scales

DYING LIGHT

Dying light   Autumnal equinox approach
and it is fitting to tie roses
          to hang and tie roses to dry
even when it's bad for my feng shui

Mix up your human parts with animals'

Ibis head and neck
Bird staff (carved)
A letter-scramble carried in a shallow dish:

Gate   wheel   speaks and entreats
Goddess of Darkness   Egyptian Venus

Rain rains   finally "on and off rain" after
"the hottest August on record"

We are equal to the animals
          shitting and pissing the plenty

Sugar ants have taken over the jade plant
and thus my money luck

CAT AT THE DOOR

Cat at the door   Hungry meow
Have to look up the word "syntax"
and aware of how often my chest
is closed   a little heart cage

The floor warms   mottled
Want to say "ringy"
and you bring me some coffee
almost as good a foreplay

"Guantanamo is the gulag of our time"

How to let love-heart energy out
give love blasts of love
          and no judgments?

We wrapped up very tightly
the baby possum killed by the cat
and put it in the garbage

HEATHER'S REAL FACE

Heather's real face popping up in the window
          Why scary-movie-frightening and seized
by lucid room spins

                                        Not wanting the dream haunting
to end   Can't see the elaborate sea dioramas
from our anchored motor boat
                                                    drifting
You have to be in waist-high water   and sea-water
    shifts around us

Yes   Micronesia *is* worried

"Out of apparent evil good will come"

2 × 11 = 22

Root

(Power in the toes)

CHERRIES

Cherries related to rose
Round and sweet like Bing
Purple-red flesh

Truck rumbles past
engine-breaking

I couldn't stay in the orchard that was really a church
in the name of poetry

You can call the daughter the mother
and the mother the child and the old people
"Big Tree Vine"

MONDAY

Monday means driving
Shit-drive   Highway to Ben White
and you on a plane seeing yellow
light and far away from me

Spring sings in February   I mean signs and
you cut the roses back
We washed by the day as
suburban urban
the grind now Tuesday
You say something about
food

HECATE DOESN'T

Hecate doesn't fucking
need you or your loving

Lovingly pull the oak seedling out
planted under mother oak
by squirrel   A squirrel joke
No just hungry squirrel
Frugal squirrel
Thoughtless thoughtless dreamy squirrel

Can't blame squirrel or oak seedling
Sad in the yard
          digging it out

Yoga pants and Hecate lochia

GRACKLES GRACK

The root of all things is green

—Arab philosopher Haley

You may present one egg
One solar sigh
Encircled Arabic #3

She laid 3 eggs
and eats the grain

The "perfect red king"
is a man becoming a woman
and bleeding every month

"Fixed with a triple nail"

This is hard work
becoming a woman

and the half-wall blocks
            what the feet are supposed to do

We have a dead elm   half chopped
3 locust trees & a sugar headache

Excuse me tree You died

You are de-limbed

Dried poppy seed pods

become petite maracas

THEY SELL YOU WHAT DISAPPEARS

They sell you what disappears   it's a vague "they"
maybe capital T   who are they and mostly
poorly paid in China

Why does this garlic come from China?
It's vague to me   shipping bulbous netted bulbs
Cargo doused with fungicide and growth inhibitor

What disappears is vague   I can't trade for much
I can cook   teach you cooking   ferment
bread or poetry   I can sell my plasma

They are paid poorly in Florida
picking tomatoes for tacos
Some CEO is surely a demon
in this poem

Need capital to buy   need to buy or else
you are always paying rent   one month away
from "the street"
3 neighbors asked for money this week
                    We are guilty
bringing in sacks of food   bought on credit

Trademark this poem   mark this poem with a scan code
on the front and digitally store it somewhere
not to be memorized “by heart”

CANCEL THAT

Cancel that wrinkle   neck crepey
What a creep in split sleeves
You can smoke tobacco   lean
winter bassy and frontal
Continental front   Blue Norther

Levittown goes "green"
Oil at $100 a barrel
January 19, 2008

You end the movie with ambient
sounds and a murder

CALM-LIVED

Calm-lived
crack the pebbles with a mallet

Maker-of-useless-things
write poems
A test for usefulness:
String a net
Pluck a bird

Call you Bird Girl and gut it

In the dream you arrive with bright
plastic toys strapped to your middle
in the kitchen

CHEMICAL COLOR

Chemical color   my nails all picky
and flake   Something more remains
like socks   cold feet   Cold
comes on icy feet   if cold could be a figure

Icy   the way I love   airy-ice   all brain

What remains does   Martin Luther King Day
        We're rhyming
Tonight we'll fuck
TV sells you things

I NEED MORE COWBELL

Come on baby
What I hear
not fearing "The Reaper"

TO EXPLODE

To explode
Head blown   a war strapped
song   We are that fracture
Rut in heat   a squeaking that
Cleavage looks like butts!
and flow my monthly courses
the Champions Sports Bar
hunger in the hugging
today   And awkward
Pink-brown   wrinkled
perfumey soap my hands are
Headache from "Gain"
The least poetic thing

A DEBT

“A debt or credit bubble”
House as weight or anchor
Pop it open like champagne
Party like that year
You can pour nostalgia
Make a depreciation
Lovely or lonely
There is no time
to slow down!
Today’s word: homeless
Homeless: home-less “without
a place to live”

WE MIGHT BE FOLDING

We might be folding laundry I am fucked
having never learned to start a fire without matches
Now I'm boy scouted   I'm cooking eggs
Are grackle eggs edible?

Stringy meat from scavengers surely

We could eat "Turks' Cap" pods or
insects   (rollie pollies?)
but there aren't enough of them either and likewise
he realizes my bee-keeping dreams are gauzy
with no uncomfortable moments
like Little House on the Prairie
the televised one   with freckles

Walk from the taco shop
with fat styrofoam boxes

I'm almost as old as Old Elvis
          without the pain pills

Should really collect shoes
of future sizes   for our boys' feet

My oven says clear/off
My toilet seats are new
& "Made in China"

For lunch
What did I have for lunch?

The boys are monitored in front
of electronics
so I could have poetry and cook

First it was too warm
and now very cold with icy threats and
The National Guard in Missouri

How Polar Bears are melting in the drowning spaces

There is no room in the shiny expensive car
to take us all to California

TOWELS

Towels What of towels
There are never enough
of them with vomit sickness
in the house

Could I clean them in the creek?

Mama?
What-a?

I need you I need something
I can't do it alone Papa Mama

What you
I love you Pooh
flying on the balloon
and spitting out bees

Triphala
how long can I store Triphala
to manage upper respiratory complaints
before it becomes pneumonia

GREAT FUNDS

"Great funds
to buy this morning"   I love:
Fridays of pizza
Something scorchy like a heater
Teaching me to fish with a paper clip
Full moon
Pointy toe shoes
Cheese and champagne
French kissing

LENSES

Lenses   Where is it
Sense of leaving before the storm noise
I can't couplet   Boat-tailed
grackle in the white-limbed sycamore

You have to send the non-baby
to the "ancestors" Scented
like blood

   I'll take sequins
dusky-rose pendants and plant them
Grow me jewels to plant
in my navel and clear out my eye crust

You can want all you want

Open the present Open it

Oya
            Winds of change   the primeval
Mother of Chaos   Queen of the Nine

Machete cuts through old growth   (sword of truth)
needs to be done

She is the wild woman
                                        Change

lightningfiretornadoesearthquakes Storms of all kinds

As the wind she is the 1st and last breath
                carries the spirits of the dead

Adept with horses   shrewd

Mother of the Mind   Warrior Queen

Shaper of storms   Fire Goddess
but also the wind

BENDY

Bendy vegetables in the drawer
behind-the-ear-cheese

Bass notes vibrate window glass

New wrinkles
Steak
Sexy skin
Stinky tea from Dr. Chung

As I come to you

Days of smithcraft
                    A fire
You have to have fire to make

GREY SLICE

Grey slice   Watch how you nourish
with your mouth corners   It's my
inner "magic tortoise"
Fortunate times around the sun
Fantastic blackout gravity everywhere
    Garlic smelling fingers

POEM

for Heather

& what's that Pisces impish look
Pour more beer in my glass   Cough
Dodge out to avoid too much eating
no clean plate   feel hunger

          I might as well say fuck it
Sing something
                    Block a bird and their rioting bodies
Slap sloping sides

Slapping overhead & traffic

I tear me to pieces   then bring them back to my face
My writing this because the dead
offer you
and what comes is this fresh young flower

The gesture from old body to young body   Identical
language of the body   gesturing
just as a hand
reaches   picks sycamore leaves

SLEEPY

for You

Sleepy and sleek
Dodging dog shit in the park
How to prevent bluntness
I adore We all together
stepping lightly
and in the airport dream: Northwest
cruddity Bean smears on the counter
of the dirty dinette

Eternal and
needy I come to you Darling
swish my underskirts
We will be
wrinkly sleep in ordinary sheets
if we're lucky Dodge a bomb
Dive to death I mean deathly we
can be alive and eat
hamburgers
drink wine

OF MERCURY

Life's message
is life   an excellent
practical joke like farts
and gurus who belly-laugh
as a daily practice

Hermes guides the dead
I slosh my feet out of the water
should learn the curative and magical
properties of plants   animals
birds and stones

Make afterlife banknotes
for your ancestors and burn them
in an impressive wad

The enclosed valley puts the letter R
in my womb
and so "into the great sea"

Your Ancient See Through (subpress, 2002)

Some poems from this publication originally appeared in the *Berkeley Review*, *The Colorado Review*, *GAS*, *Interlope*, *Kenning*, *Fence*, *Milk Magazine*, *Mungo vs. Ranger*, *Cello Entry*, *Snare*, *Lungfull!*, St. Mark's Poetry Project Online, Duration Press Online, *How(2)*, *r e a d m e*, *Transcendental Friend*, *XCP*, *The Hat*, and *LVNG*. Some were gathered into chapbook editions: *Dark* (Mike & Dale's Books), *Parrot Drum* (Leroy Chapbook Series), and *Let's Eat Red for Fun* (Boog Lit).

Red Juice (effing press, 2005)

This section originally appeared as a beautiful chapbook of the same name lovingly crafted by Scott Pierce of effing press. Some of these poems also appeared in issues of *Chicago Review*, *Baffling Combustions*, *The Poker*, *The L.A. Review*, *26*, and *effing magazine*.

Hecate Lochia (hot whiskey press, 2009)

Some of these poems were also collected in small edition chapbooks or foldouts: *Add Some Blue* (Backwoods Broadsides, 2004), *Poems* (Dos, 2007), *What Have You* (Longhouse, 2007), and *Kiss a Bomb Tattoo* (effing, 2008), and selected for print in the following anthologies: *For the Time Being* (Bootstrap), *Black Dog, Black Night* (Milkweed), *Not for Mothers Only* (Fence Books), *Poets on Painters* (Ulrich Museum), *Days I Moved Through Ordinary Sounds: The Teachers of WritersCorps in Poetry and Prose* (City Lights Foundation), and *The Volta Book of Poets* (Sidebrow Books).

Work printed here also appeared in the following journals: *Brooklyn Rail, Fence, Chicago Review, Hot Whiskey Magazine, Columbia Review, Bombay Gin, Coconut, Come Hither, Fulcrum, Poetry Project Newsletter, Mandorla, INTER, effing magazine, Pleiades, Tolling Elves, Mem, Article: Art & Imaginative Promise, The Poker, Fascicle*, and *Damn the Caesars*.

The author wishes to thank the editors and supporters of these fine presses.